Miss American Sky

poems by

Chad Hanson

Finishing Line Press
Georgetown, Kentucky

Miss American Sky

Copyright © 2023 by Chad Hanson
ISBN 979-8-88838-094-9 First Edition
All rights reserved under International and Pan-American Copyright Conventions.
No part of this book may be reproduced in any manner whatsoever without written
permission from the publisher, except in the case of brief quotations embodied in
critical articles and reviews.

Publisher: Leah Huete de Maines
Editor: Christen Kincaid
Cover Art: Cristina Conti
Author Photo: Lynn Hanson
Cover Design: Elizabeth Maines McCleavy

Order online: www.finishinglinepress.com
also available on amazon.com

Author inquiries and mail orders:
Finishing Line Press
P. O. Box 1626
Georgetown, Kentucky 40324
U. S. A.

Table of Contents

Pageants 1
CPR 2
The First Church of Transfiguration 3
Atonement 4
Local Gods #11 5
Snow = Home.. 6
Probation 7
Conch Republic 8
FREE.. 9
You're Covered 10
Totems.. 11
Triage... 12
Just Deserts.. 13
Who is the Monk? 14
Memory Foam 15
Flip Turn 16
Local Gods #17 17
The Infinite Cosmic Church Hiding Out in the Shadows
    and Silence... 18
Infectious 19
Whispers of Hymns.. 20
Dandelions / Longing / Fog 21
Here, Custer 22
Saved by the Stars 23
Escorted to Jordan by Her Own Tattoos 24
The Harpoonist in Repose... 25
Jogging in a City Park During a Pandemic 26
Polar Bears... 27
Joe Bag-a-Donuts 28
Local Gods #26 29
Horse's Mouths... 30
A Chinese Waitress at a Café on the Strip Outside of
    Tonopah, Nevada.. 31
Apparition Practice 32
He Wanted to Earn His Name 33
A Rabbit in the Navel of the Universe 34
The Master and the Oriole 35

Library of Water	36
Boarding School	37
Signals	38
Content	39
A Short Treatise on the Self as a Series of Small Fictions	40
Mirage	41
Moorings	42
Pumas	43
The Other Medicine Wheel	44
Liquid Light	45
The Woman Who Forgot to Move to Santa Fe	46
A Grackle. French Fries. The Future.	47
Ghost Dreams	48
Freshmen	49
All the Voices Make a Symphony	50
The Paisley Trout	51
Time On	52
Sing Me Home	53
A Pilgrimage of Horses	54
Lightning Trees	55
Grow Away	56
A Note for All of Us Who Grew Up Secretly Wishing to be Crucified	57
Firsts	58
Upper Peninsula	59
Local Gods #29	60
A Vision of Nectar	61
The Woman Who Married a River	62
Caught in Between Two Worlds	63
Double Feature	64
Animal Sounds	65
Wait	66
Thirsty Vessels all Around	67
The Bird that Drank the Color Blue	68
Tree Time	69
Stones	70
Miss American Sky	71
Seeing Stars	72
Acknowledgements	73
About the Author	75

*In memory of Scott King:
1965–2021
… a believer in small miracles like dragonflies,
and a generous supporter of poets from Minnesota.*

You are the sky.
Everything else is just the weather.

—Pema Chödrön

Pageants

We age slowly. We don't even
notice the changes. But the birds notice
our unraveling selves. We put on pageants
every time the sun comes up. They watch and
listen to us all. They listen like modern dancers,
laminated to the pulse. They have names for
us, but they're different. They don't use our
human names. We think we're hiding out
inside our clothes, but we live in plain
sight on the ground. Our suffering
doesn't go unnoticed. Sometimes,
with crows, they watch us so
carefully that our suffering
starts to slip up into theirs.
Since they live above us,
they see the future. That
makes them feel a solemn
kind of longing. They wish
they could pick us up and
put us somewhere else,
but they can't help.
We are too big.

CPR

Let's say we meet in a CPR course. We practice on mannequins. After we finish in the classroom, we go back to your place to practice. We practice for eight. More. Weeks. We become professionals with mad skills when it comes to blowing ourselves back and forth into one another. We blow ourselves up like a couple of balloons—taut with laughter and pink light on the inside. We float around your living room, barely even noticing the popcorn ceiling or the furniture. Sometimes I have to remind you that people die, "I mean really die, right in the middle of CPR." Then you say: "Yeah. Okay. That's true, but they never die alone."

The First Church of Transfiguration

As a way to endear himself to Ingrid, the new girl in the office, he tells her, "I know where we can find a family of blue coyotes." He explains how he found their den near the bottom of a canyon. The two of them agree to a picnic on Saturday. When they arrive, he unfurls a blanket. Then he spreads it over a thicket of grass. It's quiet in the beginning, but then the coyotes come home to their den—blue as the turquoise in a string of Pueblo beads. He points and says, "See." Then he says, "See. Look. There. See. Didn't I tell you?" Ingrid doesn't respond, so he turns to her and finds that she has become a coyote. They sit together on the blanket. No words between them, but from her expression, he can tell that it was actually Ingrid the blue coyote had become.

Atonement

Garrett spent a lifetime rustling and rounding up wild horses. Near the end, however, he started to see mustangs in a new light. He began to view them as beasts of two habitats. Hooves pressing dirt. Noses open, they turn the air into being.

On what feels like his last drive, Garrett pulls off the road to watch a band of horses on the horizon. The ridge begins nowhere and ends in the same place. Animals gliding on a seam in between this world and the next. Pounding chests and flowing manes align, riding the sky and earth, horses churning toward a keyhole.

Garrett recalls all of the mustangs that he rounded up. He pictures them in feedlots, behind bars, heads hung in grief. He wonders if the horses had been made to atone for our sins. Then it occurs to him that maybe they're the ones that left him here,

alone in a truck
to atone
for his.

Local Gods #11

This spring, Cody happened upon a god-shaped hole. He keeps falling through it on his walk home from the hotel where he works as a concierge. On one such trip he meets a woman with a pair of binoculars. She's found a peregrine. Cody steps up and asks, "Can I see?" She hands him the glass, but then she tells him: "Be *careful*." She says, "It's hard not to become a bird of prey." Cody understands what she means. He says, "Yeah. Really. The craving alone, right?" She says, "A bird is a hole. Each one, a canyon. They're all corridors." Cody doesn't hear her, though. He's already burrowed into the sky.

Snow = Home

Everybody feels defeated when it snows on May 15th. Everyone except Selma. Selma, from Oslo. She needs cold the way a salmon needs the cold. If you catch a salmon on a summer day, you can feel their desire to return to the freezing water. It's acoustic. You can hear it even though they don't make sounds. That's what it's like in Selma's house on May 15th. After breakfast, her husband tells her: "Go." Then he leads their daughter to the living room. Selma walks out into the barrage of flakes. They watch her from a window. After three steps on the lawn, it seems that she is breaking up. Selma starts to flow like

a school of plankton,
churned up and carried off by
a breeze in the sea.

Probation

After six months on the job my boss calls me to his office. He says, "Congratulations. It's the end of your probationary period." I guess I look unimpressed. He says, "Hanson. You're off probation." That really starts me pondering. Maybe as a reflex, I begin to think out loud. I say, "In truth, it's all probation," and I don't stop there: "Aren't we all on probation? I mean, the scrutiny. The conditions. The whole contingent nature of everything." I ask, "Aren't we born into this?" He says, "You're fired." That stings, at first. Then I muster the strength to channel Confucius. I tell my boss, "Yes. I am fired," then I go on. I say, "Now, please. Enjoy your probation."

Conch Republic

Greta bought a conch shell at a garage sale in Laramie. She remembered that her grandmother showed her how you can hear the ocean if you put a conch up to your ear. At home, she sat on the porch listening to the waves. She thought she heard words, too. Sentences. She spent more time than she imagined she would with the shell. By the end of the week, the phrase, "Seahorse Key," started slipping into conversations. At the table, she asked her son, "Could you please pass the Seahorse Key?" On Facebook, she typed, "He is not my Senator! I voted for Seahorse Key." After her daughter's third tantrum of the morning, she said, "If I hear one more Seahorse Key out of you girl, I'm going to give you something to Seahorse Key about." She uttered the last words anybody heard at the Post Office: "Please forward everything to Seahorse Key."

FREE

After they close the mine, his days begin to elongate. He pours alcohol over them, and they turn into taffy on a stretcher. His neck hurts. He complains to the bartender: "Coal? Who was mining who?" He answers himself, "That hole mined me for twenty years." The barkeep says, "Be happy, then. You're free." That starts him thinking. He says, "Free. Yeah, sure. I'm free." At home, in the garage, he makes a sign. He paints the letters, "F-R-E-E," on a piece of cardboard. Then he tapes it to his back. After a shot of vodka, he walks into town. A woman in a pickup truck drives alongside of him. She rolls her window down and says,
"Hey, Buddy. I'll take you."

That is not what he
intended with the sign, but
he decides: "Alright."

You're Covered

Ann grew up in Tucson. She'd never owned an umbrella. When she moved to Chicago, it didn't take long to recognize the umbrella as more than an accessory. She walked to work each day with her hand-held roof. The prospect of besting the weather made her feel happy. She started using the umbrella all the time, even on sunny days. One morning, a young woman slips up under the umbrella with Ann. They walk together for a block. They do not speak, but they smile at each other half-a-dozen times. The occasion gives Ann a chance to think hard about umbrellas. Now, once or twice a month, she finds somebody on a sidewalk that seems like they could use a ceiling. She slides up close, so they can walk in formation with the umbrella above them.

Most people smile when
she does that but sometimes they
hunker in and cry.

Totems

Two weeks after his retirement, they rush Ed to the hospital. Pains in his chest. On the table, in the ER, a team takes his vital signs. Everything seems alright, but the doctor hears a scratching sound, coming from the inside of Ed's rib cage. They sedate him. Then when they open up his chest—out leaps a badger. The physician says, "Okay. I think that was it," and all of the assistants feel relief. They set to work stitching him up, but to their surprise, a hundred and fifty moths fly down into the incision before they can finish. They ask the doctor, "What should we do?"

The surgeon grew up in the same town as Ed. He says, "It's fine," and then he starts to reminisce. "The badger served him well," he says, "You should have seen Ed twenty years ago. Stout-hearted. *Unyielding*."

After a pause, he adds: "The moths
will take him now," and then he says,
"I think Ed must belong to them."

Triage

Two years ago, the library staff noticed that patrons were not checking out any books. It started feeling like they just came to the library to talk. They stood and talked and put their hands on top of the hands of the librarians—right there at the circulation desk—were they used to scan old volumes of Virginia Woolf.

At the same time, the staff learned that some patrons were going as many as three weeks without the feel of someone else's skin touching their own. They changed their protocol up at the desk.

Charlie listens to a librarian address people at the head of the line. "What'll it be? Pat on the back? A grip on the shoulder?" He hears a woman ask, "Can I get a handshake with an extra heartfelt grab on my forearm?" The librarian whispers, "Okay, Honey." Then the woman asks, "Could you include a knowing look?" She offers the patron a soothing glance, and then she finds a soft way to say: "Yes. Of course."

Just Deserts

Julia grew up in Virginia. The thought of a desert struck fear in her as a child. Then she flew to Phoenix with her grandfather on business. Julia went to Arizona State. She spent weekends in the Superstition Mountains. Sun and rock. She began to see how the jungle of the Mid-Atlantic had made her into an actress. The desert melted all her scripts. In her apartment, she kept none of her former costumes. She started to see why the world's religions all arose out of dryness. In her senior year, Julia met a papery bartender that talked like a desert. She found books in the library that were deserts, too—entire volumes, reduced to their essence. Apart from earning her degree, on a ledge of sandstone, in the white light of our star, she vowed to become a desert herself.

Who is the Monk?

Friar Jonas leaves the monastery. He hikes to the spring pond with a bucket and a loaf of bread. When he reaches the shore, he dips his pail into the pool. Then he finds a flat place to sit.

After the ripples on the surface sink back into the water, he sees his face: receding hairline, double chin, and bags under his sullen eyes. He thinks, "Damn you, spring." There are no mirrors in the monastery. He lifts the bucket and then heads back home toward the cross atop the belfry, visible above the trees.

Before sunset, a rabbit hops up to the spring. He takes a drink, and when the waves settle, he sees himself. He shifts his weight onto his haunches. The old rabbit stays there with his water-friend. He does not wish that he was someone else.

Memory Foam

When Della starts showing signs of Alzheimer's, she moves in with her daughter, Jan. They drive to Goodwill to buy her a mattress. Della insists on memory foam. She thinks the foam will help keep her connected to the past. The bed starts working right away, but it had belonged to someone else. The events that Della recalls hark back to events in the life of the bed's previous person, an over-the-road trucker, a guy with a ham radio name: "Blackjack." Jan starts to notice her mother spitting on public streets. She rides with her window down, no matter the weather. Della struts with a new sashay, and after a lifetime of right speech, she starts to tell people to fuck themselves. Sleeping on a bed from a thrift store is a gamble. Still, Jan starts thinking she could use a mattress, too.

Flip Turn

Some of us can simply walk it off. Kai needs to swim. Even on rainy days he needs to swim. Near the end of an hour in the pool, he summersaults his eighty-first flip turn, but this time he feels something. It's a hand clasping his lower leg. As Kai completes the turn, his ankle slips through a wet cuddle of fingers. When he looks back to see what happened, he finds a woman about his age. She says, "Lightning." Then she points at the sky and hollers, "Everybody out." Kai doesn't make a sound. He stares with only his eyes above the surface. He studies her for signs, and then he sees it: the point in the future where the two of them are trees in the same forest, telling jokes the way trees do, smiling calmly with their leaves, roots knit together below them in the bedrock.

Local Gods #17

When the crow saw the kite—he knew. He recognized the sleek form as a god. He gathered his family. Then he recruited neighbors. Together they bit the string. The birds freed the deity and carried him to the top of the tallest tree in City Park. They built nests on branches in circles around the kite. For a while, they found comfort in the new god, but they also felt melancholy. Cats still killed their relatives. Food grew scarce in the winter. By the springtime, the birds began to feel like Abraham, after he pledged allegiance to the stars.

The Infinite Cosmic Church Hiding Out in the Shadows and Silence

After they deploy Rand to Afghanistan, Linda stops wearing her glasses. It feels better when she can't see things all the way. It feels like watching a film, starting somewhere in the middle. You don't know how it started. Plus, when you only see colors and shapes your eyes migrate toward the shadows. Then your ears start to prefer silence. After a while, it begins to feel like it's where she spends most of her days—in the dim light, listening to an accumulating lull. She doesn't mind, but she asks her doctor if it will lead to any long-term damage. He tells her, "No. No, not all. In fact, that's where the local gods live anyhow: in the shadows and hushes." He says, "You might as well spend time with them until Randall comes home."

Infectious

The lady up the street runs a kind of permanent garage sale. Some say it's how she infected the neighborhood. A continual stream of knick-knacks flowing out of her driveway—making their way to homes around our town. Funny thing is, the number of items at the sale never decreases. The garage stays full, no matter how many faithful shoppers come and go. I'd been scratching my head over this for seven years. Finally, my buddy explains that she reads our thoughts while we are sifting through the memories set out on rows of rickety old card tables. It takes a minute, but she figures out what we're searching for. Then we find what we needed: a tackle box that looks like your grandpa's or a hairpin like the one your mother used to wear. That's how she infects unwitting seekers with her love.

Whispers of Hymns

The first time I saw a band of mustangs,
all I could think of was my camera. I still carry a
camera and lens, but the horses showed me how
to forget about gear. They taught me to
give them my presence, instead.

For an instant, we stare at each other
through a narrow abyss. Semi-comprehending.
Each of us straining to recall the time when we
were relatives. I think out loud, "If they could
just remember." I would walk to them.
I'd whisper the old hymns
into the ears of
the horses.

Dandelions / Longing / Fog

His wife asks, "Where are you going?" Gabe tells her, "I'm taking my melancholy for a walk." She says, "Okay, Dear. Good. Give Mel some exercise." There are more cases of despair in the park than usual. It's tough to separate the personal patches of fog from the fog lifting from off the pond. At water's edge, Gabe sees a woman that reminds him of a grown-up version of a girl he used to know when they were kids. Her eyes used to see things that he couldn't see. Dandelions thrilled her, all the way through giggling—up to the point of awe. He calls to her. "Amy?" The woman changes course. He thinks, "It's true. My god. It's her." When she arrives, she tells him, "No. I'm sorry, Gabe. That person is just a story that you tell yourself." Then she bends a knee and picks a dandelion from the lawn.

Here, Custer

Come closer, yellow hair. Bring the whole cavalry.
Blue eyes. Hike them up the hill on Italian boots.
Don't forget your desires. Make sure to wear the
greed. Pack your supremacism. Put the broken
treaties in a black portfolio. Circle the wagons
and lay your traits onto the dirt in the center.
You. Handsome. Target. You.

Saved by the Stars

The police ask Abel how he got the
rocking horse onto the roof of the band
shell in the park. He tells them he, "had help."
Then he explains how it started. He lost his job.
Something switched on and all he could think of
was horses. "They're the only ones that suffer like
we do." He says, "I wanted to ride a wild horse off
of a cliff. Wind in his mane. Eyes burning like red
coals plucked from Odin's campfire. The two of
us plummeting through time and space." He
tells the officers, "I would have done it,
too, but the stars feel so much more
urgent, up there." Then he points
to the roof: "I couldn't leave this
atmosphere." One of the cops
says, "Yeah. Yeah, that's
a rocking horse."

Escorted to Jordan by Her Own Tattoos

Each one marked time. Mostly accomplishments. The
birth of a child. Her second divorce. Trips to the
Everglades. Her friends marveled at
the chapters.

When she retired, she slowed the rate at which she
added new tattoos. Then the old ones started
growing. They began to fill the space
between themselves.

On the day the stroke ended her life the
tattoos covered her. Inside the morgue,
a technician found her entirely
made out of the past. He
thought she looked
enviable.

The Harpoonist in Repose

In history class, he watches a film about Japanese ships and the science of whaling. Two days later, after a career fair in the gym, his guidance counselor asks him about his future. He tells her: "harpoonist." The counselor says, "Of course. I can see you in that line of work." He harpoons her. That's how he got a taste for the business. It's all harpoonings after that. From salesmen and county clerks to public colleges and life insurance companies. He begins to enjoy what becomes a long, happy career as a harpoonist, but by midlife his determination starts to slip off the harpoon, and onto something else. He can't see that other something, though. It's unclear. His brother asks him, "Why don't you try tending a garden?" and in so doing, he not only avoids a harpooning himself, he also saves a major part of his generation.

Jogging in a City Park During a Pandemic

At home, alone. Too long. The clock on his coffee table starts to pound. *Time. Time.* He goes outdoors, against orders. He jogs to the park up the street. On a wave of grass, time feels more like an ocean than a ticking sound. A feather falling from above. The bird's old body obeys its own version of a clock. Twisting. He stops to honor the moment—a visit from the god Chronos. He turns into a statue of himself. Then he becomes an archive, finally, a museum meant to remember the year. Sightseers no longer recall the age of the virus, but they marvel at his expression.

Polar Bears

Thirty years ago, Jed finds himself at a bar, staring into
whiskey-Seven number four. The guy next to him asks,
"What's her name?" He tells him: "Rhonda." His bar
mate muses out loud, "She sounds like a polar bear."

"Say what?"
"A polar bear."
"I don't know what you mean."
"Have you ever seen a polar bear?"
"Sure. I've seen them on television."
"What are the odds you'll end up living with a
polar bear or even spending a whole day with one?"
"Zero."
"Uh, huh. You will never own a polar bear or see
one in person. But aren't you glad they're out there?
Stalking all around? Eating up unsuspecting
people? Striking poses on the ice?
Making the color white
more beautiful?"

Jed says, "Yes. You know. I am glad they're out there."
The guy says, "She's a polar bear," and thus began
a three-decade long intoxication with wildlife.

Joe Bag-a-Donuts

The ads for Old Faithful on the sides of buses had been goading him for weeks. Joe buys a bag of donuts for the office. Then a Yellowstone-ad bus passes by, and he skips work. After a two day drive he's paying the entrance fee to the park with a bag of donuts on the passenger seat. At Old Faithful, he remembered that people take photos of gnomes in travel locations. That always struck him as odd—the garden statue as a symbol of both otherness and absence. Joe makes an image of the water spout with a bag of donuts standing in for a ceramic gnome. He visits other parks because parks serve as canvases for our stories, and also as sanctuaries from our selves. On Instagram, his colleagues notice a series unfolding: a bag of donuts in front of the country's largest redwood tree, donuts at the bottom of a cliff in Bryce National Park, a bag of donuts on a ledge above the Grand Canyon. His co-workers gather at a screen to admire the images. Then someone says: "Were those donuts for us?"

Local Gods #26

In the spring, right around Easter, some local gods started to make mischief. They were getting jealous with all of our devotion aimed squarely at the one God. Resurrection—the only miracle that anybody cites. One of them sent a plague of ladybugs, thinking that would steal some attention. We barely noticed. After that, one of the local gods changed the direction of a river. To the others that seemed like a winning approach. But alas, we live in times that vex our deities.

Horse's Mouths

Red Feather takes her out to
see some wild horses. When they find a
band of mustangs, she says, "They're more
like spirits than animals." Red nods agreement.
He says, "That's why they cannot speak anymore.
When you travel between two worlds, your words
are stripped away when you come home." She says,
"That's horrible," but Red Feather assures his date,
"It's best that they can't tell us what they know.
We couldn't even comprehend." During this
talk, the horses never break their gaze.
They remain rapt in a bottomless
cocktail: a mixture of
love-for-the-world
and quietude.

A Chinese Waitress in a Café at a Casino on the Strip Outside of Tonopah, Nevada

Long, black hair. A braid that touches
the back of her knees. She watches me
from behind spectacles.

She sets a table. Afterward, she lays a
red cloth napkin on my lap. She presses
my forehead with one hand. Then she
cradles the back of my skull with
the other. In silence, she
raises a glass up to
my lips.

I wish I could tell you the address.
I wish I could tell you the name of
the café. But I cannot. All of our
travels come to an end,
but we must find
them on our
own.

Apparition Practice

Ginny had a chance to practice as a ghost in the third day of the coma. She tried to rehearse how she would explain it to her mother. Everyone. Everything. We all lost the veneer. No one could conjure the normal, daily illusion. All of our routine haunting business became stark. Easy to see. The ghosts of old men haunting mountain lion ghosts. Ghosts with big cowboy hats haunting the ghosts of cows, and creeks, and coyotes. In the hospital parking lot, she looks up and sees a ghost of smog haunting everybody below. Skyscrapers haunting the suburbs. Still, in the middle of it all, the ghost of a girl on a park bench. The ghost of her dog at her feet. Both sets of eyes locked in tribute. The two of them haunting what's left of what they were before.

He Wanted to Earn His Name

At a workshop on cultural diversity, the dean of students introduced Ryan to a member of the Oglala Sioux tribe from South Dakota. He said, "I'd like you to meet Winona Runs-with-Deer." Ryan remembered, in the past, Native people earned their names. That made him wonder, "Who am I?" He thought his tribe might call him, "Ryan Checks-e-Mail," or "Ryan Pokes-at-a-Gadget." The seminar lasted for more than two hours. He heard four different speakers, but he did not listen to anything they said. His mind kept turning over ways that he could earn a decent name.

A Rabbit in the Navel of the Universe

Driving by my neighbor's house. I notice the youngest boy. He's motionless. Ten feet from a rabbit. The boy is six, just old enough to understand the meaning of touch. He holds his hand out to the bunny. I think to myself, "What a briskly modern composition!" The two of them frozen on the lawn. The boy does not know what is coming. He doesn't realize that time will soon drag him out onto the dancefloor. That's just as well. He is helpless to change anything: commerce, citizenship, and dry-clean-only suits. It'll be half a century before he returns to the kind of stillness that can shrink the distance between a person and a cotton-tailed rabbit. I quit driving, and for a moment it's just the three of us—the before, the before, and the after.

The Master & the Oriole

The Master and Sung-Yun went for a walk in Central Park. They came upon a group of birders with binoculars trained on an oriole.

Sung-Yun asks the Master to pause, so they can join the bird watchers in a moment of reflection—feet in the grass, eyes on the pocket-size splash of feathers. When Sung-Yun feels satisfied, they step back on the path. Then with their bodies in motion again, he asks, "Master. Why do we look at birds?" The Master says, "We look at birds because they're all that's left. The bears and wolves have been banished. The salmon are gone and we rounded up the wild horses."

The two men walk in silence until Sung-Yun finds the courage to ask, "Master. Is an oriole not beautiful?" "Yes," the Master says, "Yes," and then he whispers: "They are perfect."

Library of Water

The atmosphere holds a finite amount of water.
We have all the water we will ever have.

Each drop. Every cubic foot of mist. All of the
particles of ice. Remember.

The first drip of rain on my back porch remembers
its time as a glacier in the Pleistocene. It recalls that
it floated between palm trees as humidity in the
Caribbean. It coursed through the heart of
Robert Bennett, as a drop of blood.

In Bennett's heart the water saw a picture
of Joan, his wife, on the day that they
exchanged their vows.

Boarding School

It's the night of her first meeting as a member of the Board of Trustees. Susan dresses in business tones. She carries a tan folder with a built-in pen and pencil set. A wooden table greets her in the boardroom. When the members take their seats, the president turns on his computer and then he begins to discuss earnings.

After an hour, Gerry Becker rises. He nudges his chair back to the table, but he doesn't leave. He just stands up. Then his hips start to swing. Before long, Susan notices his pelvis beginning to swirl. His knees and elbows jerk in some kind of Trustee salsa-tango. As far as she knows, the room is silent except for the drone of the company's finances. "Can he do that?" she wonders, "What rhythm calls to Gerry Becker?" None of the other board members seem to notice.

On the drive home, she can't
remember any of the statistics, but
she recalls the dance.

Signals

After he dies, Carson finds himself in a room stocked with his favorite places. A stand of ponderosa pine outside Flagstaff, Arizona. The entrance to Yosemite, a stretch of the Oregon coast, and an island on a lake in the Boundary Waters. A voice says: "Choose." He doesn't speak. He just stares off toward the island. Now, families camp on Carson's shore. They build fires, and when they do, they use tee-shirts and paper plates to send smoke signals into the atmosphere. They don't know why, exactly. They tell each other they feel, "moved," but the signals are Carson's means to let the world know he still has something to say.

Content

Jared spends his life in front of a monitor. He stares at content all day long. Then he goes home to watch a television, but tonight the city is holding a Christmas parade. He buys a soft pretzel. Then he sits on the curb to wait.

Floats begin to roll down Collins Avenue. He looks at the colors. People cheering. After the fifth float, a man in a Santa suit walks passed, surrounded by a group of women dressed as elves. Jared realizes something. He's wearing a Santa hat. He stands and walks into the street. For the first block, he's just an office worker in a fuzzy hat. By block two Jared starts to turn into somebody else. He imagines himself as a drum major in a marching band. Jared's spine arches backward and his feet shoot out into the air in front of him. When it feels right, he waves to onlookers. After three blocks, it occurs to Jared that he is the content now.

He doesn't know if
that is better, necessarily,
but it feels like a start.

A Short Treatise on the Self as a Series of Small Fictions

To remember something afterward. Do we unearth our recollections? If so, from what earth do we excavate? Do we dig our dreams out of the soil? Or, do we author them? Is each one of us a library, with stacks arranged on scaffolds from the land of biograph? Is that landscape a body of water? A watercolor? *The way the winter light arrives on the necks of herons.* Do we trick sunbeams the same way that we trick the light out of each other? Shaking hands, facing the void, in the showrooms of car dealers? "Don't look down," they always tell you. I'm not sure that is good advice. Why not chisel the history that we lay at our heels when we walk? What if we could all agree

to just drive around
in wheat fields, as opposed to
racing to the end?

Mirage

No one on the road construction crew could remember a hotter June. Each day the sun cooked the land into ghosts. Mirages. There and then not there. One day, Bailey watched a mirage go to work as a solvent, canceling the ground. Erasing history. The future, too. Last week, the heat felt like a blanket covering the land, only to lift and reveal a more elegant version of the place. Bailey started to look forward to the mirages. She anticipated the annulment of the countryside. She remembered, somebody once told her, knowing that a thing will go away makes falling in love a necessity.

Moorings

I noticed, after the doctor told her about the cancer, Wendy started buying calendars. Little page-a-day numbers that rest on countertops. Datebooks and schedules with faux-leather covers. Big, showy wall calendars, too. She uses an upscale pen to write on them: meetings, events, and projects. At one point, I tell her, "You seem really busy, Wendy. Busier than ever." She grew up sailing. She says, "The future is a string of ports, spreading out toward the west, along the shores of time. Berths and jetties. Wharves and docks. Dependable places to moor yourself." I'm sure I look confused. She says, "Writing on a calendar is casting a line. It's extending a rope out to a time that's still to come." Her words stop me in the water, and for a moment—I just float.

Pumas

The Bureau of Spirits hired a panel of historians to find out when the clouds started to take on the shape of mountain lions. In an official sense, the sightings did not pose a threat, but when the cougars started to stalk commercial airliners, the Bureau felt compelled.

The scholars traced the first appearance to an event in Oregon. A rancher used a team of dogs to tree the last mountain lion in North America. Then the coward shot the puma with his rifle braced on the hood of his pickup truck. A story in the local paper said, "The lion didn't fall." The author went on to say, "the cat seemed to rise up," and he added that the rancher, "left the scene confused."

The Other Medicine Wheel

On Sunday, she drives up to see the Medicine Wheel: a six-thousand-year-old circle, made out of stones set in the dirt. She tells her boss, "I went to the *Medicine Wheel!*" He says, "Oh, yeah. That's for tourists. It's not the real Medicine Wheel." Then he draws a map. A week later, when she finds the other wheel, she pitches a small tent. She looks at the stones until after dark. Then they start to look at her. After generations spent standing in for history—a folded paradise—the wheel can see a future at last, but it's a future that won't come.

Monday morning, she walks out her door with a cup of coffee. On the lawn, she finds the medicine wheel. It followed her home. She drops the mug, but she doesn't feel startled for long. After dinner, in the grass, she starts to learn all of the ways that stones can hope.

Liquid Light

This year, on his summer vacation, Tim flew from Pensacola to the Marquesas. He booked a guided trip to fish in the mangroves. The day after he lands, in three feet of water, on the bow of a boat, with a fly rod in his fingers, he becomes a little overwhelmed. Water in every direction. Not just water. Every drop in the sea swirls with a dance partner—a particle of light. He doesn't see the ocean so much as he feels it in his cells. Back at home, he tells a doctor, "Everything I look at appears to me as a liquid." The physician writes him a referral to an optometrist. On the walk from the office to his car, Tim sinks up to his knees in the parking lot. He pauses a moment. Then he slips fully into Bay Street and he starts swimming toward the blue glow in the Gulf.

The Woman Who
Forgot to Move
to Santa Fe

Jenadene had lived like everybody else: work, followed by a couple of hours of TV, followed by sleep. Repeat. Caught in the middle of the routine, time appeared to her as a monolith—the past, present and future all vibrating as a block.

After Jenadene retired, she noticed time beginning to delaminate. Entire years started to come undone. Now, in the morning, between six-thirty and eleven, she strains coffee through the layers. Yesterday, she excavated the summer of 1998, a time when she thought she might move to New Mexico. She couldn't remember why she didn't move to
the Southwest. She also wondered
if there was time left
to rebury what
retirement and
coffee had
unearthed.

A Grackle. French Fries. The Future.

Someone threw a half a bag of fries out of their car,
onto my lawn. A grackle finds them. I watch the bird
from my window. He pecks at the fries. Without self-
consciousness. He plucks and hops around. He eats
and eats. He is not making plans for his retirement.
When he finishes, he flies to one of the branches on
my neighbor's apple tree. He cleans his feathers.
He's not wondering if he will outlive his money.
He shuts his eyes. A breeze tickles his feet. He
doesn't see death coming at him like a train
chugging out of the future. He just sits on
a branch in my neighbor's apple tree.
Sitting.

Ghost Dreams

After the sun dance, a Cheyenne elder explains to Red Feather, "If you wake up from a dream before it reaches the ending, the dream becomes a ghost. It keeps on dreaming, even during the daytime." He says, "Your ghost dreams, and those of others, all of them out there. Together. In the street, at the office, on the countertop in the kitchen."

The words were meant to serve as a warning, but Red Feather did not take them that way. For Red, the thought of his unfinished dreams ghosting around in the daylight, beside others, made him feel more like a member of the tribe.

He tells the elder, "They're unfinished, and they lost their dreamer. That's too bad. I understand." Then he says something in a tone that sounds like someone he is meeting for the first time: *"They have each other."*

Freshmen

Once a week, during his first semester of college, Nathan hikes to a rock quarry with a speaker he plugs into his iPhone. Through the speaker, he plays the impossibly sentimental tunes of John Denver, the kind of songs everybody feels ashamed to like. He sets the speaker at the water's edge, and then he climbs a cliff. He sucks in a long, high-diver breath. When he begins to fall, *fear* drives away all his other feelings. He falls through awkwardness, anxiety, and embarrassment. Then he falls out the other side. Before his feet hit the surface, he hears the purest kind of music from the speaker—the kind of sound that can bust a cloud or even kill someone. John Denver doesn't bust or kill Nate, however.

The song just
makes the water
feel like home.

All the Voices Make a Symphony

For the first fifty years of her life, choir
practice felt like going to the gym. Routine.
Obligatory. But lately, choir practice feels like
a date at a spa, the type where you look forward to a
soothsayer laying hands all up and down your spine.
Lately, choir serves as a massage, the sort where your
normal aches soften and float up out of your skin into
the air around your body. Today, when she stands with
her sisters, voices interwoven in the atmosphere, it
feels like maybe there are stories that don't even
come to endings. It feels like they're standing
there, inside a chamber that keeps growing,
and not in a linear way. Just opening.
A billowing out in every direction
… like the universe.

The Paisley Trout

A hippy girl in Montana dropped a hit of acid
into a stream coursing through a meadow in the
Cabinet Mountains. An old man rainbow trout
gobbled the hit. It transformed him. Paisley.
Painted on his scales, up and down his sides,
along his back, and all over his tail.

He swam downstream. He thought
he might try to find himself
in the retro galleries of
the new West.

Time On

During his career in the city, Roger used coffee to vault himself onto his calendar. The days stood still, but Roger flew. He hurtled himself through time like a blue javelin. Then his boss explained how the company, "didn't want to," but they needed to, "downsize." Roger sold his loft in Denver's hippest neighborhood. Then he bought four acres in New Mexico. Now it's Roger that's unmoving. He stands at the edge of his garden watching the sun come up over the Sangre de Cristo's. It's time on the move now, but the hours do not crash by him like waves, rushing toward the shore.

The days well up slow
like the burgeoning tide of
an estuary.

Sing Me Home

They spend a week packing their belongings into boxes that they picked up at a liquor store. On the day the lease expires they put their things into a trailer. Then they start off toward the coast. Halfway there, a light on the dashboard tells him that the trailer has come free. In his rearview mirror, he watches it flip and bounce. Clothes, books, and dishes scatter onto a field.

He feels an impulse, but he doesn't pull over.
Both of them know the song on the radio.

Of all the land mammals
we are the only beasts that
sing to each other.

A Pilgrimage of Horses

Red Feather leads a trail ride. Seven travelers and seven downhearted ponies. The forests of Wyoming unfurl beside them. At a vista, he stops for photographs. One of the travelers, a girl, asks: "How many people come here to ride horses? He tells her, "thousands." Then she asks, "Do the horses like to give rides?" Red says, "Creator gave my people horses at a time when we were sad. He gave us ponies as a way to make the darkness shine." Red Feather tells her, "Look at these horses. They are sad all the way to the edge of their bodies, but they carry on." Then he says something, half to the girl and half to the animals: "These ponies. They are not sweating. They glow."

Lightning Trees

For generations, the oak in Ginn's Field served as a lightning rod for the county. Tall branches to goad the weather. Roots sunk in a deposit of ore. After Susanna died, the black river of his thoughts carried him to the tree in the middle of a storm. He hugged the broken bark and prayed, but the tree would not abide. Nor would the heavens. He slept at the base of the trunk, under a canopy of leaves. When he awoke, he found his thoughts still careening, but the current didn't run so dark. When he sat there unmoving

he could see past the
surface into the depth of
the water column.

Grow Away

Jason feels bitter-sweet on the day he drops his
daughter off at the dormitory. Eighteen years of
childhood struck him as a sentence in the beginning.
Now it feels like the end of a vacation that he
had been looking forward to.

At home, his posture starts to change. Jason's back
sags under the weight of his shoulders. He takes the
clock off of the kitchen wall and throws it in the
garbage can behind the house.

After lunch, he remembers his grandfather's old
hourglass, stored in the attic. He puts the
timepiece on the coffee table in the
living room, but he doesn't
turn it upside down. He
likes the white sand
better when
it's still.

A Note for All of Us Who Grew Up Secretly Wishing to be Crucified

It started with piercings. Then it moved across the street into tattoo parlors. "You bet it hurts!" We enlisted an army of skateboards. They put elbows in casts and stitches in chins. We suffered well. We served our pain up as an offering—a way to heal the world.

Fifteen years into careers, we begin to figure out it doesn't work. The whole thing starts to feel like some kind of a trick. They taught us how life and the cosmos unfold as transactions. "This for that," they said. The lesson made working for a paycheck seem palatable, but life is not an act of commerce. Neither is the universe. Consider grass. Or chipmunks. Most of everything you know.

Last year, I met a woman. She urged me: "Let's all pretend that we're chipmunks, quietly liking one another and snacking on things that grow out of the ground." In contrast to our culture of markets and exchanges, her words struck me as a reasonable kind of prayer.

Firsts

She saw her first mustang eight years ago. She named him Cimarron, so he could live on in her mind after he ran away. On weekends, she looks for him in the dryness of the Red Desert. Her friends think the search is part of a moral task, an honorable cause. She disagrees. She explains how she has seen a thousand horses in the time since Cimarron. She admits, they're all majestic. She can see them in her memory. They're striking, but they're blurry. In contrast, her image of Cimarron stays married to the first realization that we share this planet with free-roaming bands of horses. A moment of insight can become a rascal. In this case, the moment parked alongside Cimarron. The instant of discovery has spent the last eight years working to sharpen up his silhouette.

Upper Peninsula

Road construction in upper Michigan didn't feel like a dream job, but he needed work. Friday, at dusk, a van pulls up to a cross in the ditch. With an orange "Slow" sign in his hand, he watches six people hike to the cross. In between words on a walkie-talkie, he watches them circle the marker. They make a loop that seems like part of an old Finnish rite—a grief dance. The folks in the ditch form a knot and then they begin to smolder. They look like they're privy to a piece of knowledge uncovered by first-man and first-woman. They are locked in zest. He watches as they turn into a tribe. The grievers appear to him as natives, set loose from a painting by Matisse. The next morning, he drives passed the site and wonders:

how do we know
what happens to us
isn't good?

Local Gods # 29

After his first week on the oil patch outside of Williston, Gary starts searching for local gods on his iPad. It takes a while, but he finds a retired surf god that had come home to North Dakota. On Sunday he takes a dirt road, and in time he locates the god on the porch of a farmhouse. They make small-talk. Then Gary asks, "Do people worship you somehow?" The god says, "No … no. I'm not that kind of god," and then he adds, "I'm more the type that just grows old. Now I serve as a reminder." They talk for fifteen minutes. Then Gary stands up and says, "Thank you." He starts his truck and puts it in motion. Behind the wheel, he finds himself in the position of observing the moment that he is living through.

He really *hears*
the squeak of tires on
the gravel road.

Visions of Nectar

Bud and Clare are sitting at the picnic table when the season's first hummingbird arrives. The bird floats in front of Clare. In a yard full of green, no blooms in sight, the bird inspects her hazel eyes. She watches him. He hums to the left and the right, unable to discern between her irises and nectar pushed into the world by spring. He sticks out his tongue, as if the space in front of her could offer a taste of syrup. Clare turns to Bud and says, "Did you see that? A hummingbird just about drank one of my eyes." Bud says, "No." She rebukes him. "What do you mean? You're sitting right here? He flew up and nearly drank my eye." Bud tells her, "Yeah. I didn't see that." Then he contemplates. "It might have been his appetite you saw." Hummingbirds send hunger out ahead when they come home.

The Woman Who Married a River

Her mother and her older sisters spoke about the water in hushed tones. They whispered to rapids and eddies, so she grew up in thrall. As an adult she leaves her apartment at night. The river looks forward to her. She sets her clothes on shore and presses her body upstream. Backstroke. When she grows tired, she changes direction. Face down, now. The river holds her on the surface. To swim is to fly. Afterward, on the sand by the bank—she waits. Over the years, it started taking longer to dry off. She doesn't remember when it started. Sometime after she turned forty? A circle

on her ring finger
stays wet. A bead of water
flowing all the time.

Caught in Between Two Worlds

Carl's grandfather died. His friends notice, in the weeks after the funeral, Carl starts to speak with something more than the accent that's common in South Dakota. It sounds like something closer to broken Swedish. His friend Mary makes an observation: "You talk like your grandpa, now." Since it's the first time that it's been drawn to his attention, Carl doesn't have a comeback. He just denies the claim. Then, later on, something occurs to him. He's been spending a lot of time with his grandfather in the weeks since he died, to the point where Carl can barely tell if he's standing in the past or the present. During the confusion, he's been picking up his grandpa's tendencies.

Double Feature

She walks in the door at 11:30. He asks, "Where have you been?" She says, "I don't know." He asks, "What do you mean?" She looks sincere. She tells him, "Some days you make two movies. The first one is familiar. The second one has subtitles. It's missing the continuous, moment-by-moment tissue of reality that holds the story together. It's hard to tell what the hell is going on a lot of the time—but it's actually a better film." He shrugs disapproval. She says: "I wish I could tell you more. It's not the kind of feature that I ever planned to make."

Animal Sounds

When the cabinet factory placed him on furlough, Adam started to spend a lot more time outdoors. He spent more time outside in a week than he'd spent in the last eight years. He noticed things. The sweetness of the air. Tall blades of grass going to seed. He began to look at the elements differently. The water from his faucet became a clear-running stream. Each lightbulb in his house, a tiny sun. His neighbor had to listen hard, but she thought she heard him making animal sounds. Grunts and screeches, mostly. In one case, a quiet howl. The time he'd wasted on the assembly line started to feel like an abomination. When the letter comes, telling him to return to his job, he *hisses* at the envelope.

Wait

Their friends thought the two of them had aged well together. They had learned the trick of how to wait. For years, they'd waited for their kids to start lives of their own. They waited for each other in doctor's offices. They waited till they had enough money to retire. Now they're waiting to die, except they're not waiting anymore. Neither one of them awaits. Since the end involves no anticipation, they just walk around the senior park, fully themselves. Earl and Karla. The days lap over them like water on the shore of Lake Huron

each swell dampening
their rocks and sand, making them
feel saturated.

Thirsty Vessels All Around

When she lost her husband, Caroline turned into a cup with a crack that extended from lip-to-base. Her life story leaked out every day. Her identity dribbled through the crack until, by the middle of the morning, she sat empty. Six months into her life as a widow, she notices that time—ordinarily the enemy—starts to take her side. Something that looks like silver solder starts to fill the crack at the base of the cup. To her surprise, it holds tightly. Now, she's full all the way to lunch, through dinner and on into the evening. At first, she fears the soldered crack will define her: "This woman was broken." Of course, that's part of the meaning, but the silver also serves as a fine compliment. She's become the cup that people reach for when they find themselves caught in the grip of thirst.

The Bird that Drank the Color Blue

A Hopi woman in a café once told me that Eagle loved the sky. She said he needed blue so much, the sky was not enough. He came to earth to drink the color. He drank blue from spruce, waters, and mountainsides. Finally, when he felt full, he took to a perch on a ridge above the desert.

Soon, Eagle came to know that when he drank the color blue, he also drank in our sadness. More than he could hold. The bird's life passed from him, and his feathers began to fall. One by one they lilted down over the world. Where they landed, the stones that cradled them became turquoise.

Tree Time

On the third day of spring I sit under a crab apple tree watching buds attempting to bloom. In between bites from off of a sandwich, I focus my attention on a single bud. I'm hoping to see, and I'm imagining, the moment when it bursts, but I'm running out of lunch hour. We are accountants when it comes to time. My ledger slips into accounts-no-longer-receivable. No bloom. I'll tell you. Trees. They don't obey. They recognize no intervals. They don't devour time the way we do, with all of our clocks.

Trees animate time
—a crab apple surfing through the
curling infinite.

Stones

Minneapolis. It's winter. Jared's home from his last tour of Iraq. Mostly he's been sitting on the porch in a tee-shirt. After three weeks, his wife sends him to a psychologist. The shrink asks the usual questions. Then, without a prompt, Jared starts telling a story. He tells about how he used to remove stones from his father's fields when he was young. He describes how frost used to push the stones up from the soil, to the surface. He tells the doctor, "I picked up some stones in Iraq. Real heavy ones. I was hoping the cold would drive them out." The doctor says, "*Right.* Right. Yeah. Our bodies don't work like that." He pat's Jared's knee and says, "You are not a wheat field, my friend." Then he explains that we do not expel our stones. He tells Jared, "We have to wear them down and sweat them out." He prescribes a course of Nordic skiing through the winter, and by the springtime, Jared feels about as light as he did before his deployment.

Miss American Sky

This year, a 27-year-old waitress from the Bronx shows up to compete for the title of Miss American Sky. The officials tell her it will not be easy, but she stays. She goes up against the southern sky. She vies with the Aurora Borealis and a storm in the desert. When the waitress presents herself, the judges have to squint because she's tiny. Still. They take the time. Skies are astute. They spend eternity looking down at us. When the judges study her, they can tell, two rivers of tears have poured from her eyes. They agree. Hardship has made her kind, so they ask one of their assistants to put a tiara on her head. Then they give her a hug of rain.

Seeing Stars

For most of his life, Lou
assumed that starfish were more like
plants than animals. Then he saw a TV
show about them. The show included time-
lapse video: life sped up by degrees. The starfish
crawled all over the seafloor and each other. They
didn't strike Lou as plants *or* animals. They struck
him as people, reincarnated as stars. Now, when
he gazes at them on the shore, he has an easier
time enjoying their company. When he finds
two stars clinging to one another on the
bed of a tidepool, he recognizes that
they're two old prize-fighters,
wrapped in a moment of
gladness, heads on each
other's shoulders, after
the sound of the final
bell has ended their
time in the ring.

Acknowledgements

I am grateful to the editors of the following publications, where earlier versions of these poems appeared:

> *Flyway:* Miss American Sky
> *Matter:* The Paisley Trout
> *Stone Gathering:* Atonement and Triage
> *Eastern Iowa Review:* Local Gods #11
> *Z Publishing Anthology*: Library of Water
> *The Dewdrop*: Jogging in a Park During a pandemic
> *Pittsburgh Poetry Journal:* CPR
> *PROEM:* Seeing Stars

In addition, many of the poems herein were included in a chapbook: *… people just float …* published by Kallisto Gaia Press.

I am also indebted to the Wyoming Arts Council. I enjoyed the support of a creative writing fellowship, granted by the kind and dedicated staff of the WAC, during the time that I composed a portion of this work.

About the Author

Chad Hanson serves as a member of the faculty in Sociology and Religion at Casper College. He is also the author of several books, including *In a Land of Awe: Finding Reverence in the Search for Wild Horses*, and two collections of poems, *Patches of Light* and *This Human Shape*. In addition, he is co-founder of the Wyoming Mustang Institute, which works through research and advocacy to ensure healthy and stable wild horse populations on public land.

For more information, visit: chadhanson.org.

www.ingramcontent.com/pod-product-compliance
Lightning Source LLC
Chambersburg PA
CBHW030224170426
43194CB00007BA/852